How To Teach
The Five-Paragraph Essay

By David Dye, M.ED.

This book is dedicated to my fellow teachers.
There is no group of professionals I respect more.

For workshop / staff development information call
(562) 627-5662 or go to CreateBetterWriters.com.

Model Citizen Enterprises
12 W. Mesquite Blvd. Suite 108
Mesquite, NV 89027
CreateBetterWriters.com

ISBN: 0-9766146-8-5

Table of Contents

Introduction

There are many ways to write a five-paragraph essay. Consider this: There are four domains of writing. Also, within these four domains of writing there are sub-domains such as problem/solution, persuasive, letter writing, personal narrative, biography, autobiography, cause and effect… I could go on and on. In addition to this, every person has his or her own distinct style of writing. With all of these factors to consider, it's no wonder that so many students struggle with essay writing.

Don't let all of this intimidate you. This book is going to show you how to teach the five-paragraph essay using one simple essay format. From this basic format, you will discover that adjusting it to fit the different domains of writing is very simple. More importantly, your students will feel confident in their ability to write in any situation.

ONE SIMPLE FORMAT

This book is going to take you by the hand and show you how to teach the basic five-paragraph essay using one standard format. Following these easy steps, your students will achieve mastery of the five-paragraph essay and be prepared for ANY timed test you, your district, your state, or college throws at them.

BELLS AND WHISTLES

Everyone likes the machine with extra bells and whistles. This book will also show your students how to add the "bells and whistles" to their five paragraph essays. Once they've mastered the basic format of the five-paragraph essay, they will learn important ideas such as Interesting Introductions, Smooth Transitions from paragraph to paragraph, Classy Conclusions, and much more. If you are teaching fourth graders, only a few bells and whistles will be needed. However, if you are teaching middle or high school, you will have all the resources you need to help your students write sophisticated essays. Once again, they will do this by adding these "bells and whistles" to a basic, easy to use five-paragraph essay format.

THE NEXT LEVEL

Before discussing the next level, let me tell you about a common mistake used with essay writing. Many teachers will write a five-paragraph essay, such as a persuasive argument, with their class. Next, they will write a narrative with their class. Next, they will write a problem-solution, cause and effect, or compare-and-contrast essay with their class. At the end of the year, their students have wonderful, finished essays to show parents, administrators and the district. What they DON'T have is a class full of students who know how to write the five-paragraph essay all on their own.

Isn't our goal to help students achieve <u>mastery</u> of the five-paragraph essay? If the students are relying on the teacher to walk them through the process, have they really mastered it?

So what is the next level? The next level is the ability of the students to take the basic format of the five-paragraph essay and "tweak" it to fit any domain of writing. By "tweaking", I mean simply adding an extra step or two to meet the requirements of the assignment. For example, essays are not generally stories. However, by "tweaking" the outlining/prewriting procedure for the five-paragraph essay, they can change the body of the essay into the beginning, middle, and end of their story. As you will see, this is a very easy thing to do.

THE FORMAT OF THIS BOOK

1. List of Steps – First you will receive a list a steps to follow when teaching the five-paragraph essay. This will serve as an overview as you get comfortable teaching this process. Also, you can use this as a guide while actually teaching the five-paragraph essay.

2. Sample Pacing Chart – From Day 1 to Day 20, what will your daily lessons look like? Obviously it will vary from grade and ability level. However, it is nice to have a model to use as a starting point. Using this pacing chart you will find that speeding up or slowing down is easy. Simply take more time to complete each step or jump to the next step when you feel your students have understood each lesson.

3. Detailed Lesson Plan – Next, each step will be explained in greater detail. You will see pictures and receive a detailed explanation of each step.

4. Plan for Total Mastery – The goal is to have every student master the five-paragraph essay. This lesson plan will show you what to do with the students who have mastered the skill, and how to find time to work in small groups for those who continue to need support.

5. Bells and Whistles – Now you will learn to teach your students how to make more exciting introductions, classy conclusions, smooth transitions, and more…

6. The Next Level – Show your students how to use the basic format of the five-paragraph essay to create any domain of writing. Does your district give your students a timed test on persuasive letters? Are your students required to take a state writing test on problem-solution? Not a problem. In minutes your students will know exactly what to do to create any genre of writing.

THE FIVE PARAGRAPH ESSAY

I. The Steps

1. Review "What is a Paragraph?" Make sure the students understand that a paragraph is about ONE MAIN IDEA.

2. Teach the Three-Paragraph Essay in 60 seconds. Start your watch! Ready…Set…Go!

3. Prewriting Practice for the Three-Paragraph Essay. Creating your Three Main Ideas and listing your supporting details for each.

4. Introduction Paragraph – Make a thesis statement and give your three main ideas.

5. Conclusion Paragraph – Summarize your thesis statement, review your three main ideas, and say goodbye.

6. Putting it All Together

7. Timed Prompt Writing

8. Assess and Re-Teach as needed. Put the expert essay writers into "writer's workshop" activities while working with those who need a little more help.

Bells and Whistles

1. Teach Interesting Introductions

2. Teach Classy Conclusions

3. Teach Terrific Transitions

The Next Level – Tweaking the Essay to Fit All Domains and Genres

1. Narratives

2. Persuasive Essay

3. Problem-Solution Essay

4. Cause and Effect Essay

5. Research Reports

CreateBetterWriters.com

THE FIVE PARAGRAPH ESSAY
II. Sample Pacing Chart

From Day 1 to Day 20, what will your daily lessons look like? Obviously, it will vary from grade and ability level. However, it is nice to have a model to use as a starting point. Using this pacing chart, you will find that speeding up or slowing down is easy. Simply take more time to complete each step or jump to the next step when you feel your students have understood each lesson.

Day 1 – Paragraph Review

1. Review the five parts of a paragraph using the pretest.

2. Practice memorizing the parts of the paragraph.

3. Practice prewriting the paragraph. Topic: A Good Book.

4. Home Work (H.W.) Memorize the five parts of the paragraph.

Day 2 – Paragraph Review

1. Game: How fast can you say the five parts of the paragraph. Time several volunteers. Reinforce that a paragraph is about ONE MAIN IDEA.

2. Review the prewriting from yesterday. Write the paragraph together.

3. Students prewrite a new topic on their own. Topic: A Funny Story

4. H.W. Write the paragraph to "A Funny Story"

Day 3 – Topic / Closing Sentence Review.

1. Review the five parts of a paragraph – Test tomorrow.

2. Discuss how topic sentences explain the one main idea, closing sentences summarize the one main idea.

3. Add topic and closing sentences to "A Funny Story" and "A Good Book".

4. H.W. Prewrite and write a paragraph. Topic: The Perfect Pet.

Day 4 - Paragraph Test

1. Prewrite and write a paragraph.
   Topic: A Funny Character in a Story

2. On the back of their paragraph tests, have them list
   the five parts of a paragraph.

*Note: Do NOT go on until most of your students have mastered the paragraph
and CLEARLY understand that a paragraph is about ONE MAIN IDEA.

Day 5 - The Three-Paragraph Essay in 60 Seconds.

1. Teach the concept of a three-paragraph essay in 60 Seconds.

2. Practice prewriting the three/five paragraph essay. Students set up their paper
   to include the topic on the top and the three main ideas on the left margin.
   Train them to do this automatically whenever they hear that they will be required
   to write an essay.

3. Begin prewriting the three-paragraph essay. Find three main ideas and list
   supporting details for the topic: Your Favorite Day of the Week

Day 6 - Prewriting Practice

1. Review the three-paragraph essay in 60 seconds lesson.

2. Practice finding three main ideas for four other topics from Appendix 1.

3. Begin learning to list 5 to 7 supporting details for each main idea.

4. H.W. Find three main ideas for sixth topic.

Day 7 - Prewriting Practice

1. Practice listing supporting details for all six topics.
   Focus on keeping details short.

2. H.W. Finish prewriting for all six topics.

*Note: Do NOT go on until most of your students have mastered prewriting the
essay. Give more topics if needed. Practice setting up the paper, finding three
main ideas, and listing supporting details until most of your class can do it.

Day 8 - The "Boring" (but well-organized) Introduction Paragraph

1. Memorize the parts of an introduction paragraph.

2. Practice writing thesis statements with your six topics.

3. H.W. Give students three topics. Have them write a thesis statement for each.

Day 9 - The "Boring" (but well-organized) Introduction Paragraph

1. Review the parts of an introduction paragraph.

2. Write a "boring" introduction together as a class using the six topics that have already been prewritten. Reinforce that the outline (3 main ideas) is the prewriting for your introduction.

3. Students write two introduction paragraphs.

4. Include closing sentences in these paragraphs.

5. H.W. Write two more introduction paragraphs.

Day 10 - Interesting Introductions

1. Review introduction paragraphs. Have the students write the introduction paragraph to the sixth topic.

2. Review Types of Introductions. (See Appendix 5)

3. Complete Interesting Introductions worksheets. (See Appendix 6)

4. H.W. Finish Worksheets

Day 11 - Interesting Introductions: Comma, Comma, And... Thesis Statement

1. Review Types of Introductions. (See Appendix 5)

2. Begin the Comma, Comma, And... worksheet. (See Appendix 7)

3. H.W. Finish the Comma, Comma, And... worksheet.

Day 12 - Interesting Introductions

1. Students will attempt to change their six "boring" paragraphs into interesting introductions using the Comma, Comma, And... strategy.

2. H.W. Continue to work on changing boring introductions into interesting introductions.

Day 13 - "Boring" (but well-organized) Conclusion Paragraphs

1. Memorize the parts of a conclusion paragraph.

2. Write a conclusion paragraph together using Conclusion Starters.

3. Students write conclusion paragraphs for the six essay outlines.

4. H.W. Continue to work on conclusion paragraphs for the six essay outlines.

Day 14 – Interesting Conclusions

    1. Review the parts of a conclusion paragraph.

    2. Review the Comma, Comma, And... Introduction Paragraph.

    3. Have the students rewrite their boring conclusions using the Comma, Comma, And... strategy.

Day 15 – Timed Five-Paragraph Essay Test

    1. Write a Five-Paragraph Essay. To help students move through the essay, put pacing chart on the board.

    2. Write finish times on their rubrics. Use the rubric to score their essays.

    3. H.W. Write an essay. It is due in one week.

Day 16-20   Review of Five-Paragraph Essay

    1. Students who passed the five-paragraph essay can work on "Bells and Whistles" activities, Writer's Workshop type activities, or other projects assigned by teacher.

    2. Review the steps of the five-paragraph essay.

    3. Second timed test. Use rubrics to score their essays.

Day 21+   Plan for Total Mastery

                        CreateBetterWriters.com

THE FIVE PARAGRAPH ESSAY
III. Detailed Lesson Plan for Each Step
Step I – Review the Paragraph   (Approx. I Week to 3 Months)

Make no mistake, the ability to write a strong paragraph is the very backbone of all writing. If your students cannot write a good paragraph, trying to write an essay will be futile. On the other hand, if your students can produce a well-organized paragraph, the battle is nearly over. Writing a five-paragraph essay simply requires a few extra steps.

For a more detailed lesson plan on paragraph writing, go to CreateBetterWriters.com. You can download the paragraph lesson plan from the "Past Newsletters" section of this site. Below you will see an abridged version of what you will find in How To Write a Paragraph.

> There is one all-important, vital, key, pivotal main idea that your students must have on their minds at all times when writing the paragraph (and consequently, the five-paragraph essay. That one main idea is this:
>
> A Paragraph is about ONE MAIN IDEA!

This point could not be stressed strongly enough. Pound it into your students' minds every chance you get. To not do this is to make your job teaching the five-paragraph essay infinitely more difficult. Here are the steps for teaching the paragraph:

1. Pretest: Let the students try to guess the five parts of a good paragraph.

Write numbers I – 5 on the board. Have the students number I–5 on their papers. Let the students try to guess the five parts of the paragraph. Make a game out of it. Offer five raffle tickets or a small prize to the student who can name the #I part of a paragraph. (List is in order of importance.)

A GOOD PARAGRAPH
1. One Main Idea
2. Topic Sentence
3. 5–7 Sentences
4. Closing Sentence
5. Indent; Spelling and Punctuation

Offer four raffle tickets for the student who guesses the second item and so on. The class will have fun, and it will get them thinking about everything they've ever been taught about writing. This is a great time of review, even if they don't discover all five. For the classes that aren't coming close, I'll give as many hints as I can until they get it.

When finished, now is the time to start pounding into your students' brains that a paragraph is about ONE MAIN IDEA. I'll do "call-and-response" over and over: "What is a paragraph about?" The class will respond, "ONE MAIN IDEA". Look each student in the eyes and ask, "What is a paragraph about?" The student responds, "ONE MAIN IDEA". Ask them during math, on the way to lunch, and when you see them on the playground. It should become a reflex, like when a doctor taps your knee with that little hammer. A paragraph is about ONE MAIN IDEA!

2. Memorize the five parts of the paragraph.

Make your students commit the five parts of the paragraph to memory.

3. Prewrite and Write a Paragraph Together

Select an easy topic such as "A Good Book". Review with the students that there are hundreds of MAIN IDEAS from which to choose. However, they can only select one main idea. Once they have chosen their main idea, think of five supporting main ideas for that one main idea. Have them set up their paper this way:

<u>Before Prewriting</u>	<u>After Prewriting</u>
Topic	A Good Book
One Main Idea: 1. 2. 3. 4. 5.	One Main Idea: Cat in the Hat 1. A bored boy and girl home alone. 2. The Cat comes to play 3. They have a lot of fun 4. They destroy the house 5. They clean the house just before mom comes home.
Write the Paragraph Here	Write the Paragraph Here

Use this prewriting format to write your paragraph. Now that you have selected your one main idea and you've listed your supporting details, writing the paragraph is easy. Be sure to work on topic and closing sentences as you write the paragraph together.

Depending on the age and ability level of your students, the time needed to teach the paragraph will vary. Do not shortchange this step. Spend as much time on it as you need to make sure it is mastered. Create a list of topics for your students to practice. Use topics from social studies, science, and your literature series to help practice the paragraph. Once the paragraph is mastered, you're ready for the next step.

<u>Step II</u> – Teach the Three-Paragraph Essay in 60 seconds. Start your watch!
   <u>Ready...Set...Go!</u>   (Approx. 5 min.)

When your students can organize a paragraph by writing their
one main idea, listing their supporting details, and writing it using topic and
closing sentences, they are ready for the three-paragraph essay.

This is my favorite part of the entire process. It's fun, and it builds their confidence. They
know how long it took to learn the paragraph. Telling them that they are going to learn the
three-paragraph essay in just one minute, will make them very eager to learn.

1. Begin by telling your students how good a teacher you are. You are so good that you
   are going to teach them the three-paragraph essay in 60 seconds. You can even set
   your watch to it.

2. Three-Paragraph Essay in 60 seconds. Start your watch! Ready...Set...Go!

   Teach the three-paragraph essay by asking a series of questions:

   A. Ask your students: "What is a paragraph?" (By now you should have drilled it
      into their brains that it is about ONE MAIN IDEA!) Remind them if necessary.

   B. If I ask you to write a ONE-MILLION Paragraph Essay, how many main ideas
      will you need?   (Answer: One Million)

   C. If I ask you to write a ONE-THOUSAND Paragraph Essay, how many main
      ideas will you need?   (Answer: One Thousand)

   D. If I ask you to write a ONE-HUNDRED Paragraph Essay, how many main ideas
      will you need?   (Answer: One Hundred)

   E. If I ask you to write a TEN-PARAGRAPH Essay, how many main ideas will you
      need?   (Answer: Ten)

The Grand Prize Question:

If I ask you to write a Three-Paragraph Essay,
how many main ideas will you need?

The Answer: THREE!!!

Congratulations, you just learned how to write the Three-Paragraph Essay.

A three-paragraph essay is just three paragraphs
about a topic. Therefore, simply think of three main ideas
about the topic, write the paragraphs, and you're done.

Step III – Prewriting Practice for the Three-Paragraph Essay. (Approx. One Week)

Tell your students that, from now on, forever and ever, when a teacher asks them to write an essay, they need to format their paper doing the following*:

A. Write your topic on the top!

B. List your three main ideas!

C. List your supporting details for each of the three main ideas.

*This is just like the paragraph.

If your students learn to set their paper up just like this, even before they hear the topic, they will automatically be reminded of the steps involved in writing a five-paragraph essay.

Notice, in the top circle, they will write their first main idea. In the second circle, they will write their second main idea, and in the third circle, they will write their third main idea.

Their 5-7 supporting details will be listed around each circle. *Once mastered, the average fifth grader should complete this prewriting in about fifteen minutes. By timing your students, you train then not to drag their feet throughout this process.

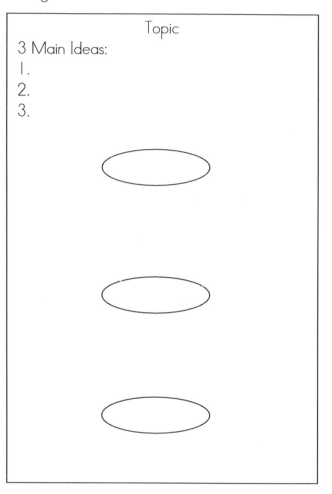

Prewriting Practice – Listing the Three Main Ideas:

See the list of Five Paragraph Essay Topics in the appendix of this book. Give the students a topic. As a class, think of three main ideas for that topic. List the three main ideas on the paper.

Example:

My Favorite Day of the Week
Saturday

3 Main Ideas:

1. No School

2. Play with Friends

3. Our family has "Family Night"

CreateBetterWriters.com

Prewriting Practice – Listing the Three Main Ideas: (Cont.)

Believe it or not, this will be the hardest step for many students. Coming up with three main ideas for a topic can be extremely difficult. Take your time and make sure they feel comfortable with this step.

A. Have students cut three sheets of paper in half. Choose six topics from the appendix or on your own. On the first half page, have them format their paper. Tell them, "You are going to write an essay…" Pause… Wait to see if anyone formats their paper correctly. Tell them, "I'm waiting to see if you remember how to format your paper…" A few will clue in that you are waiting for them to write:

```
3 Main Ideas:
1.
2.
3.
```

Once they figure out that you are waiting for them to format their paper, they will begin to do it automatically each time you write.

B. Have the students come up with three main ideas.

Issues to discuss while working on this step:

- Select three main ideas that are related. Don't select three main ideas that have nothing to do with each other. For example, if the topic is "My Favorite Day of the Week", you could use Saturday: 1. No School; 2. Play with my friends; 3. I was born on Saturday.

  Which one of the three main ideas does NOT belong? #3 I was born on Saturday. The first two are about activities, but the third is about something else.

- Do NOT list the topic as one of the three main ideas. This is a very common mistake. The students need to be trained to put the topic at the top of their paper immediately when they hear it. The three main ideas explain the topic.

- Each main idea should be something that would make a good paragraph. If they cannot think of 5-7 things to say about it, have them select a different main idea.

C. Repeat steps A and B with five more topics. Have the students use half sheets to save paper. They can practice formatting on the front and back of each paper.

Prewriting Practice – Supporting Details

Your students have six topics, and you've found three main ideas for each. Now, practice listing supporting details for each main idea. Out of the six topics you've already done, practice listing supporting details for two of the topics as a class. Use the other four topics for independent practice. Below is a sample for Favorite Day of the Week. See the appendix for several samples of actual prewriting outlines written by students.

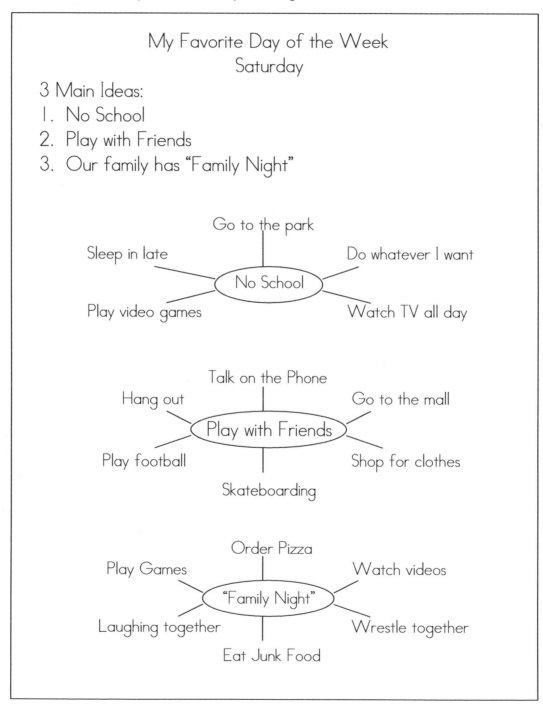

My Favorite Day of the Week
Saturday

3 Main Ideas:
1. No School
2. Play with Friends
3. Our family has "Family Night"

Go to the park
Sleep in late — No School — Do whatever I want
Play video games — Watch TV all day

Talk on the Phone
Hang out — Play with Friends — Go to the mall
Play football — Shop for clothes
Skateboarding

Order Pizza
Play Games — "Family Night" — Watch videos
Laughing together — Wrestle together
Eat Junk Food

Step IV - Introduction Paragraph (Approx. One to Two Weeks)

1. Teach the parts of an introduction.

Begin by teaching the parts of an introduction. Make them memorize the parts and have them practice every day. It's fun to make a game out of it. Ask volunteers to say the three parts as fast as they can. Time them and put the fastest time (usually around 2-3 seconds) on the board.

> **Introduction**
>
> 1. Make a Thesis Statement
> 2. State your Three Main Ideas
> 3. Make a Transition Statement

This would make a great poster to put on your bulletin board.

2. Practice writing <u>thesis statements</u>.

Simply put, the thesis statement explains the topic of the essay. I tell my students to "punch your reader in the face with the topic of your essay." Don't beat around the bush. Come right out and say the main purpose of the essay. It doesn't have to be fancy, just come out and say it.

Examples:

Expository: "Saturday is my favorite day of the week."

Persuasive: "Every fifth grader should be able to go to camp."

Cause and Effect: "The American Revolution was a direct result of British tyranny."

Problem Solution: "Feeding the homeless would be much easier if we all work together."

Narrative: "Under attack, the king had only one last chance to save his kingdom."

** By now you have made six outlines. Train your students that the TOPIC is the inspiration for the thesis statement. Look at the six outlines, have the students look at the topics and write thesis statements for each. Remember, punch the reader in the face with the main idea of the essay.

CreateBetterWriters.com

<u>Introduction Paragraph (Cont.)</u>

3. Write a "boring" introduction together as
   a class.

   Remember this:

My Favorite Day of the Week
Saturday

3 Main Ideas:

1. No School

2. Play with Friends

3. Our family has "Family Night"

Important: This part of the students' prewriting IS the prewriting for the Introduction and Conclusion paragraphs. If they did this step correctly, writing an introduction (and conclusion) paragraph is easy.

*Write the introduction together as a class. Each main idea from the outline becomes a sentence in the introduction. End with a transition sentence that summarizes the topic.

Example:

Saturday is my favorite day of the week. There is

Main Idea #1 ◄──── no school on Saturday so I get to do whatever I want. Saturday

Main Idea #2 ◄──── is also my day to play with friends. Finally, on most Saturdays my

family gets together for "Family Night". Saturday is a day I look

Main Idea #3 ◄──── forward to all week.

Note: Many students will want to put supporting details in their introductions. Tell them to save the supporting details for the three body paragraphs.

This kind of introduction may not be exciting, but if your students are writing these kinds of introductions, at the very least, they are well-organized beginnings for their essays.

** Your students have written six thesis statements. Use these to practice writing introductions.

CreateBetterWriters.com

4. The Comma, Comma, And ... Introduction.

Later in the book we will discuss interesting introductions. However, now is a good time to show your more advanced writers how to spice up their introductions.

Let's review the three main ideas of the "boring" introduction for Favorite Day:

1. No School   2. Play with Friends   3. Family Night

Notice that the <u>comma, comma, and</u> ... represents a list. Your students will simply make their thesis statement followed by a list of their three main ideas. Here's a sample:

Saturday is my favorite day of the week because there is <u>no school, I</u> can play with my <u>friends, and I</u> get to enjoy Family Night.

Your students can begin or end their introductions with the comma, comma, and... Now they have the rest of the introduction to get the readers attention.

Every person has a favorite day of the week. Some people get excited about Mondays because it's the start of the week filled with so much potential. Many people like Wednesdays because it's "over the hump" day. Others like Friday. Their work week is ending and they have all week-end ahead of them. For me, there is one day of the week that gets me more excited than any other. Saturday is my favorite day of the week because there is no school, I can play with my friends, and I get to enjoy Family Night.

Appendix 7 has a wonderful worksheet titled the Comma, Comma, And.. Interesting Introduction. If you feel that your students are ready for it, now is a good time to teach it.

Here is a sample of a paragraph that uses the comma, comma, and... introduction at the end. Notice how the beginning of the introduction prepares the reader for the essay they are about to read.

Introduction Paragraph (Cont.)

As a class, we wrote a sample essay outline for "What I Want To Be When I Grow Up". We wrote the "boring" introduction together, then used it to write a more interesting introduction. Here is what our boring introduction looked like. The students generated the sentences.

Boring Intro
When I grow up I want to be a teacher. First, I just love working with children. Next, it would be a great job because I would enjoy learning with them. Finally, I would have summer vacation for the rest of my life. What more could you ask for.
_____
Interesting Intro:
Thesis Statement because

Next, I had the students write interesting introductions for their own essays. Here is a sample of one fifth grader's essay. Notice how he does not use "because". Rather, he turns his thesis and three main ideas into two sentences.

When I tell you what I want to be when I grow up, you're going to think that I'm crazy. Everyone I tell always says the same thing, "Give it up. It's never going to happen." They're probably right. I'm not very strong or fast, but I'm pretty good at it already. When I grow up, more than anything else, I'd like to pitch for the Los Angeles Dodgers. They are my favorite team, I love playing the game, and I'll become filthy, stinkin' rich.

** For practice, students can turn their "boring" introductions from past essays into interesting introductions.

Step V – Conclusion Paragraph.   (Approx. One Week)

Before starting the conclusion paragraph, notice how we have not practiced writing the three main-idea paragraphs. If your students can write a paragraph, there is no need to spend too much time writing these paragraphs. At this point, you may want them to write the introduction and three main idea paragraphs for homework. However, it might be more productive to spend your precious classroom minutes on the conclusion paragraph.

The Conclusion Paragraph

The process of writing the conclusion paragraph is the same as writing the introduction. The only thing that changes is the attitude. With an introduction you are preparing the reader for your topic. With a conclusion, you are reviewing the topic. That's the only difference.

CreateBetterWriters.com

Conclusion Paragraph (Cont.)

** Write a conclusion together as a class following the steps below. Most of the steps should sound familiar.

1. Memorize the parts of a conclusion.
   Hint: They are the same as the introduction.

2. Use the list of "Conclusion Beginnings" below to help your students transition into their conclusion paragraphs. Have students take their thesis statements from the past six essay outlines, and make them summarize each statement in three different ways using the conclusion starters below.

Conclusion
1. Summarize Thesis Statement
2. Review your 3 main ideas.
3. Give final thoughts/opinions.

5 Paragraph Essay

Conclusion Starters

As you can see...

It is clear that...

Without a doubt...

Most would agree that...

As you now know...

It is easy to see that...

Certainly...

Clearly...

Obviously...

Surely...

Indeed...

Examples:

1. As you can see, Saturday is my favorite day of the week.

2. Without a doubt, Saturday is my favorite day of the week.

3. Clearly, Saturday is my favorite day of the week.

3. Now, use your old essay outlines to practice writing conclusions. Remember, that the prewriting / outline serves as your prewriting for the introduction and the conclusions paragraphs.

   Note: Your conclusions can be short and sweet. Simply summarize the thesis statement, review your three main ideas, and say goodbye.

Conclusion Paragraph (Cont.)

Here are two sample conclusion paragraphs. The first shows the "boring" approach, the second uses the comma, comma, and... style.

Boring Conclusion

As you now know, I would like to be a teacher when I grow up. When I'm a teacher I will get to be creative. I will also enjoy the challenge of teaching. Finally, I know that my love for children will make the job a lot of fun. I cannot wait to get started.

Once again, the "boring" conclusion may not be exciting, but it is well organized. For many students, this will be a fantastic accomplishment.

Comma, Comma, And... Conclusion

It is easy to see that being creative, enjoying the challenge, and loving kids will make teaching a lot of fun. Many teachers say that if they could do it all over again, they would still choose to be a teacher. I'm sure it will be frustrating at times, but I couldn't image doing anything else. Teaching will give my life meaning, and it will provide me with many blessings. I look forward to many years in the classroom.

Here is another sample of a conclusion paragraph my class and I wrote together. I kept it up on the bulletin board as we worked on essay writing to help reinforce this key element of essay writing.

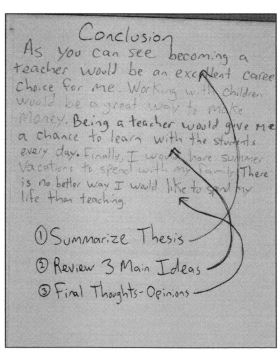

CreateBetterWriters.com

Step VI – Putting It All Together.

Your students now know everything they need to write a clear, well-organized five-paragraph essay. Follow the suggestions below to help keep this skill fresh in their minds.

1. Require your students to write a five-paragraph essay every week.

   a. Monday = Make an Outline

   b. Tuesday = Write the Introduction and Paragraph #1 of the body.

   c. Wednesday = Write Paragraphs #2 and #3 of the body.

   d. Thursday = Write your conclusion.

   e. Friday, in class, assess each other's essays.

2. Use topics in other areas of the curriculum to write essays. Suggestions:

   a. Response to Literature   (Example: Write a five-paragraph essay about how different personalities in the story affected the plot of a story.)

   b. Social Studies Topics   (Example: Write a five-paragraph essay about the causes of the American Revolution.)

   c. Science Topics   (Example: Write a five-paragraph essay about three ways that rocks are formed.)

   d. Book Reports   (Example: Write a five-paragraph essay about the book. Main Idea #1 – Summary of the Story, Main Idea #2 – Describe your favorite character, Main Idea #3 – Describe your favorite scene in the book.)

3. Have the students assess each other's essays. Use the Five Paragraph Essay Assessment Sheet (Appendix 3). The students will check for the key elements in each other's essays.

4. The next sections will discuss timed writing to a prompt. This is a key step in mastering the five-paragraph essay.

CreateBetterWriters.com

Step VII – Timed Prompt Writing.

Timed writing to a prompt has become the preferred method of assessing student writing skills in many states and districts. This is a good reason to train your students to complete all the steps in just over an hour. Many district and state tests give the students an hour to write with a ten minute opportunity to prewrite. This will serve as our baseline for student mastery of the five-paragraph essay.

The image to the right is a rubric that can be used to chart every student's progress for every detail of the essay. In order to pass the essay, they need to successfully complete each step within 70 minutes. If your students can do this, there will be no doubt

> ### Five Paragraph Essay
>
> When you finish your essay, attach this to your work.
>
> _____ 1. Five-Paragraph Essay Prewriting. (8 out of 10 needed to pass.)
>
> _____ 2. Introduction Paragraph   (8 out of 10 needed to pass.)
>
> _____ 3. Three Main Idea Paragraphs   (12 out of 15 needed to pass.)
>
> _____ 4. Closing Paragraph   (8 out of 10 needed to pass.)
>
> _____ 5. Completed Essay in 70 Minutes.   (4 out of 5 needed to pass.)
> 60 minutes or less = 5 pts.
> 60 – 70 minutes = 4 pts.
> 70 – 80 minutes = 3 pts.
> 80 – 90 minutes = 2 pts.
> 90 + minutes   = 1 pt.

that they have mastered the five-paragraph essay.

Your students' chances for success will increase greatly if you practice timing them on each step AS YOU TEACH IT. For example, while I'm teaching Step III – Prewriting, I'll practice timing them. I'll give them fifteen minutes to complete the task. After fifteen minutes, announce that those who are finished will easily pass this step on their essay tests. Those who are not finished now know that they need to work harder.

In order for a student to pass the five-paragraph essay in seventy minutes, they need to be able to do each step in the follow time amounts:

Prewriting = 15 – 20 minutes

Introduction Paragraph = 10 minutes

Three Main Idea Paragraphs = 25 minutes

Closing Paragraph = 10 minutes

Quick Edit / Revision = 5 – 10 minutes

The Rubric

_____ 1. Five-Paragraph Essay Prewriting. (8 out of 10 needed to pass.)

When you score the prewriting, you're looking for three good main ideas listed in an order that makes sense and that they've listed at least five details for each main idea. If they make minor mistakes, but the overall prewriting is good, you can give them 8, 9, or 10 points. These are passing scores. If they do not pass, list the items that need work on the rubric.

_____ 2. Introduction Paragraph   (8 out of 10 needed to pass.)

Is there a good thesis statement? Does it list the three main ideas? Does it have a good transition sentence? If it is acceptable, give them 8, 9, or 10. If not, list the problems they have made on the rubric.

_____ 3. Three Main Idea Paragraphs   (12 out of 15 needed to pass.)

Each paragraph is worth five points. If each paragraph has a good topic sentence, supporting details, and a closing / transition sentence, it should receive at least 4 points which is passing.

_____ 4. Closing Paragraph   (8 out of 10 needed to pass.)

Does it summarize the thesis statement? Were the three main ideas summarized? Do they end the essay with a closing statement?

_____ 5. Completed Essay in 70 Minutes (4 out of 5 needed to pass.)

After giving your students a topic, start the timer. As each student completes their essay, record their time on the rubric, circle the time window (i.e. 60–70 min.) and put their score on the rubric immediately. If they complete the essay in seventy minutes, they pass the timed portion of the test.

Step VIII – Assess and Re-Teach

What do we do with the students who don't pass? It's true that some students, depending on the age and ability level, will need to be taught this skill every year. However, many students WILL get it if they are given small group instruction with the teacher. The problem is that most teachers simply don't have the time to re-teach all of these steps individually to their students.

There are a couple of ways to create blocks of time to help students master the five-paragraph essay. First, if you have <u>The Complete Writing Program</u> (available at CreateBetterWriters.com), you already have a resource in place that will help your better writers advance to the next level. With this program, the students will automatically identify the strengths and weaknesses within each other's writing. If a student forgets any of the steps in essay writing, another will be there to point it out. The students will be on automatic pilot, leaving you to work with the students who need more help.

The second way to create a block of time is to give the students who passed the five-paragraph essay one assignment while you work with those who didn't pass the essay. Have them do Writer's Workshop type activities, book reports, etc... The next section will give you a more detailed plan of a project you can do with your students that will serve the needs of all your students.

The Five Paragraph Essay
IV. Plan for Mastery

As stated in Step VIII of the Detailed Lesson Plan, you can create a block of time for you to work with those students who need additional help with the five-paragraph essay. This section will give you a plan that will help most of your students master the essay. Any student who fails to master the five-paragraph essay after this is either deliberately not trying or is not ready to internalize this skill.

1. Begin by teaching the five-paragraph essay to the entire class. When you sense that a large portion of your class understands the five-paragraph essay, give a timed test. The students who receive a "Pass" according to the rubric are ready to move on.

    There have been years when I have been able to give the first timed test after a week. The students understood the prewriting, introduction, and conclusion immediately. I gave the test and over half the class passed.

    Other years, it is weeks before the class is ready for their first timed test. Each class, as well as each student has their own personality. This is why teaching is an art as well as a science. You'll just have to "feel" when they're ready. You'll feel it because you'll be checking their work as you go.

2. Dividing the Class
    A. Put the students who pass on one side of the room and the students who continue to need help on the other side. Ask the students who passed to make a list of ten (10) topics that they could use as writing ideas. These could be stories or essays. When finished, have them prewrite and write their first essay or story.

    A second option is to give them some of the worksheets from the "Bells and Whistles" section of this book. They can work on improving their introductions, conclusions and transitions while the others work on mastering the essay.

B. Re-teach all of the steps involved in the five-paragraph essay.

1. Pass back the rubrics from the first timed test. This will show them what part of their essays still need work. When you are teaching a step which they did not pass, this will help them know that this is a skill needs extra attention.

2. Re-teach the prewriting, introduction, and conclusion. Give a second timed essay test. Complete the rubrics the same way you did it the first time.

   By now you should have well over half your class passing the essay. The new students who have just passed the essay can join the others in the writing activity. The students who are left usually fall into two categories:

   a. Those who are not passing because they are still confused about the steps involved with essay writing.

   b. Those who are not passing because of issues unrelated to essay writing. They may have language barriers or processing problems. In this case, simply reinforcing how to organize one paragraph would be considered a success.

   In either case, the following project will give you the time you need to work with each of these students. You will be able to give them individual instruction that will help take them to the next level.

The Five-Paragraph Essay Project

1. Give the students a list of five topics. They will write a five-paragraph essay for each. Use the topics to the right or select your own.

2. Give each student a rubric. Have them write "Essay #1" on the top. Have them write the date and time they start each step next to the step on the rubric. These students tend to be slow and normally are not self-starters. By writing down the times they begin, you can keep track of the amount of work they are doing.

Essay Topics
1. What I like about my school.
2. The best way to spend a day off.
3. How to _____. Select something you know how to do.
4. What I would change about myself.
5. A place I would like to visit.

3. The students begin by prewriting the first topic. As they complete their prewriting, they must bring it to you for inspection. If they did the prewriting correctly, write their names on a master sheet stating that they have passed the prewriting. They never need your

4. signature for prewriting again.

However, if they are not prewriting correctly, conference with them, give them a mini-lesson, and have them do the prewriting again. They need to bring it back for inspection.

Note: You may want to have a sign-up sheet if you start getting students lining up. You can call them when you are ready. Allow them to go to the next step until you are ready to conference with them. Also, at the end of each day, collect what they've done and check it. This will save time the next day.

5. Repeat the process above with the introduction, body, and conclusion. The students will work through each topic until they have mastered each step.

6. When a student has passed all of the steps without your help, he/she is ready for a timed test. Have the student do the next topic on the list or give him/her another topic from the list in the appendix. Time him/her and score the essay.

Final Thoughts

Many teachers have a Writer's Workshop type program in place that allows them to conference with students on an ongoing basis. Whatever program you are using, save the students' rubrics from their five-paragraph essays. The odds are that no matter what you do, there will be a few students who will need to work on the essay all year. Use the rubrics to track their progress. You can also pass the rubrics on to future teachers. It will help new teachers know right away what areas require help.

THE FIVE PARAGRAPH ESSAY
V. Bells and Whistles

Interesting Introductions

In the detailed lesson plan, you were shown how to write a well-organized, but less than exciting introduction. You were also shown how to use the Comma, Comma, And... strategy. The worksheets that follow will help you take the Comma, Comma, And... strategy, and use it to make interesting introductions.

When using the Comma, Comma, And... strategy, the student frees up the rest of the paragraph to get the reader's attention. The picture to the right shows students creative ways to use that extra space.

The following worksheets are in the appendices. Use them to help your students learn to write better introductions.

> Interesting Introductions
> 1. Tell a Story
> 2. Attention Getter
> 3. Strong Opinion
> 4. Question
> Advanced
> 1. State a Fact
> 2. Give a Statistic
>
> End with Comma, Comma, And...

Worksheet #1 – Interesting Introductions

Types of Introductions

Tell a Story: A short three to four sentence story that helps prepare the reader for the topic.

   Sentence Starters: "I'll never forget the time when..."
      "I'll always remember the time when..."
      "There was a special time in my life when..."

Attention Getter: Any statement that makes the reader want to read more. Examples include making a gross, scary, or exciting statement.

   Sentence Starters: "You'll never believe what I'm about to tell you."
      "If I could go back in time, I never would have..."
      "It was the most painful thing that I've ever felt."

Strong Opinion: Give an opinion that leads into your thesis statement. Your goal is to make people want to respond.

   Sentence Starters: "I firmly believe that..."
      "No one will ever convince me that..."
      "There is only one opinion that an intelligent person can conclude when..."

This worksheet (Appendix 5) lists the six different types of interesting introductions. Give each student a copy and use it to help the students complete the other worksheets. The teacher may want to make a poster out of it and post it in the classroom.

CreateBetterWriters.com

Worksheet #2 – Comma, Comma, And...

Use this worksheet to help your students practice putting their thesis statement and three main ideas together. They will select a thesis statement and three main ideas for each topic. Next, they will practice writing a Comma, Comma, And... sentence.

Worksheets #3 and #4 – Identifying Interesting Introductions #1 and #2

Discuss the six types of interesting introductions with your class using Interesting Introductions (Worksheet #1.) Next, read the introductions as a class and decide what kind of introduction is being modeled. It is important to note that these paragraphs are samples. Have the students save these worksheets in a writing folder. Whenever they finish prewriting a topic, have them review the three worksheets before they write. This will give them ideas to spark their creativity.

Next, use Worksheet #2 – Comma, Comma, And... to practice writing their own interesting introductions. Have them write two different Interesting Introduction paragraphs using each thesis statement. Take advantage of the fantastic feature on Worksheet #1 which give students "Sentence Starters". These are great ways for students to get accustomed to using these types of introductions.

Classy Conclusion

In a standard five-paragraph essay, a simple summary of the thesis statement and review of the three main ideas is fine. However, adding a little creative flair wouldn't hurt. This can be achieved just by having the students practice rewriting their introductions.

Do you remember the difference between the introduction and the conclusion? Basically, it's the attitude the writer takes when writing them. The introduction introduces the essay. The point of view the writer uses stresses that the reader is about to receive information.

In the conclusion, the point of view of the writer is to summarize. The writer has already given the information and is bringing the essay to a close. Therefore, the introduction is going to be re-written, only from a different point of view.

What to do: Have your students complete the Comma, Comma, And... worksheets from the appendix. If they practiced writing Interesting Introductions, have them rewrite the paragraphs. However, tell them to pretend that the essay has already been written and now they are writing the end of the essay. Challenge them to think of an interesting way to bring their essays to a conclusion.

Terrific Transitions

Students need to be trained to develop smooth transitions between sentences and paragraphs. The worksheets in the appendix will help you do this. Keep in mind that when your students finish writing their essays, looking for good transition words and phrases should be a regular part of the revision process. Train your students to identify the key elements of an essay as they assess each other's work. Additionally, they should be checking for transitions as well.

Worksheets: Transition Words #1, #2, #3 and #4

A well placed transition word can mean the difference between a smooth essay and an essay that the reader must struggle to read. These worksheets will give your students several suggestions on good transition words and help them practice incorporating them into their writing.

Worksheet Transition Sentences

When writing a five-paragraph essay, one of the first things that your students will do is find three main ideas. These main ideas should be related somehow. The worksheet (Appendix 9) will ask them to end a paragraph by showing how an idea in one paragraph is related to the main idea of the next paragraph.

When your students have completed the worksheet, have them go back to their old essays and revise them. Have them add transition sentences to their first two main idea paragraphs. This will be an excellent way to help them develop this important skill.

THE FIVE PARAGRAPH ESSAY
VI. The Next Level

"The Next Level" Oooh! It sounds so formal. However, when you think about how the five-paragraph essay is set up, how much effort does it really take to alter it to fit nearly any genre of writing? In this section we will look at a few types of writing and see how the prewriting can be adjusted to fit that genre.

The key is the prewriting. If you set up your essay correctly, the hard part is over. Therefore, I will show you how to adjust your prewriting for several genres of writing. You can then show your students. Remember, the key is to set up your prewriting appropriately.

First, let's review how the students prewrite the five-paragraph essay.

My Favorite Day of the Week
Saturday

3 Main Ideas:

1. No School

2. Play with Friends

3. Our family has "Family Night"

Remember, the students write the topic on the top. Next, the student thinks of three main ideas that support the top.

For each genre of writing, the three main ideas will need to fit the type of writing the student is doing.

Here are some examples:
(These would make great posters for your bulletin boards.)

Narrative (Story): The three main ideas would be:

1. The Beginning of the Story
2. The Middle of the Story
3. The End of the Story.

Definition: A narrative tells a story. It can be written from the writer's point of view (1st person) or the writer can describe things happening to others (3rd Person). A narrative has a beginning, middle, and an end and includes several elements of a story. These elements include a conflict, rising action, and a resolution. Throughout the narrative, characters are developed, themes are presented, and the reader is entertained and enlightened.

Persuasive Argument: The three main ideas would be:

1. Reason for Change #1

2. Reason for Change #2

3. Reason for Change #3

(An explanation of the topic that needs to be changed should go in the introductions. Refuting the counter argument can go in the conclusion or main idea #3)

Definition: In a persuasive argument, the writer is trying to convince someone that his or her point of view is correct. The goal is to persuade the reader to agree with the writer. In a persuasive argument, the writer not only wants to list reasons for the change, but they also want to refute any counter argument the reader or an opponent might have.

Problem–Solution Essay: The three main ideas would be:

1. Clearly State the Problem

2. Solution #1 or (#1 and #2)

3. Solution #2 or (#3 and #4)

Definition: A problem–solution essay has a clearly defined problem and gives clear solutions for the problem. The goal is to fix the problem by presenting clear evidence that the writer has the solution. The writer's goal is to make it obvious that his or her solution is the best.

Cause and Effect Essay: The three main ideas would be:

1. Completely describe an important event.

2. Explain the cause of the event.

3. Explain the effect of the event.

Definition: A cause and effect essay does what it says; it explains the cause and effect of a major event. The goal for the cause and effect essay may be to explain why important events occurred and the impact they have on other events.

CreateBetterWriters.com

Research Report: The three main ideas would be:

1. 1st most important feature of the topic.

2. 2nd most important feature of the topic.

3. 3rd most important feature of the topic.

Definition: The goal for the research report is to become an expert on a single topic. The writer uses his or her expertise to inform the reader about important information on a topic. While reading about the topic, the writer will list facts until three important main ideas appear. They then focus their energy finding information on these three main ideas.

The Essay Portfolio

This is a great project if you want to blow parents, other teachers, and administrators out of the water with your class's fantastic essay writing. Begin the project by saving your students' essays throughout the year. Make sure they've written at least one essay from each genre. Cover pages are in the appendices for each genre listed in this section. Have the students write a quick explanation of the genre on the cover page (you can copy the definitions of the genres in this sections), then place the final draft of the essay behind it. Have the students make a nice cover with a title and their names. This is a project that is guaranteed to impress all those who see it. Follow the steps below to help complete the project:

1. After teaching the five-paragraph essay, begin doing an essay for each genre listed.

    a. Review the type of writing. Go over the definition of the genre (see the previous section for definitions).

    b. Have the students write the definition of the genre in their own words on the cover pages (see appendices).

    c. Write the five-paragraph essay. Make sure they produce a nice final draft.

    d. Save their essays for the project.

CreateBetterWriters.com

<u>The Essay Portfolio – Cont.</u>

2. Design a Cover – After the student has written an essay for each genre, begin making the books. A suggestion for a title might be:

My Essays
(Insert School Year)

by _____

The students are free to decorate the cover with pictures related to writing (pencils, paper, etc...). They can even list the genres on the cover surrounded by fireworks, banners, or other decorative items.

3. Make a table of contents

4. Organize the table of contents and the essays. Secure them into the folder.

CreateBetterWriters.com

Appendices

Five Paragraph Essay Topics

1. Your favorite day of the week.

2. If you could choose any occupation for your future, what would it be?

3. If you could go to any amusement park, which one would you select and why?

4. Describe why you would or would not like to be a <u>pirate</u>. (Cowboy, Astronaut, etc...)

5. What would you do if you won the lottery?

6. If you could have one wish, what would it be?

7. If you could meet anyone in the world, who would it be?

8. Describe the perfect friend.

9. If you could be anyone in the world, who would it be?

10. Describe the perfect day.

11. Everyone knows how to do something. Describe something you know how to do.

12. How kids can change the world.

13. Describe the perfect vacation.

14. If you could change one thing about your school, what would it be?

15. What advice would you give a new student at your school?

16. What would you like to be when you get older? Describe three things you will need to do to accomplish that goal.

17. Describe the perfect pet.

18. If you could visit any place in the world, where would it be?

CreateBetterWriters.com

Sample Essay Outlines

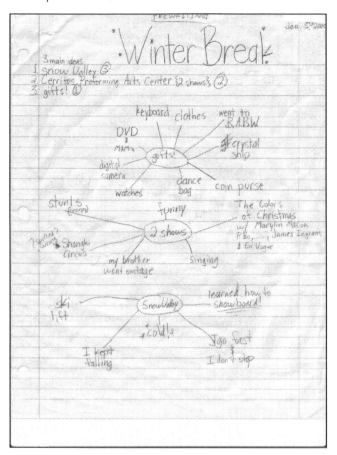

Notice that this student has listed her three main ideas. Next to each main idea, she listed a number. After writing her three main ideas, she decided that the first main idea should go last. See the "3" circled next to "Snow Valley." She also decided that her third main idea should be first so she put a "1" next to it.

Notice that Jay has listed five supporting details for each main idea. He has not written complete sentences. He just writes enough information to help him remember his details when he gets to each point in his essay.

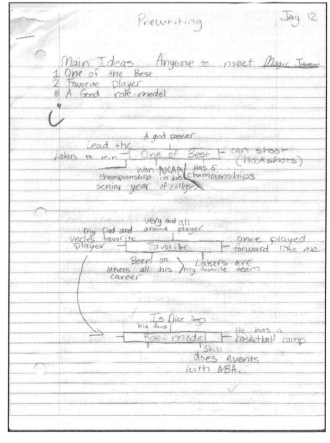

CreateBetterWriters.com

Your Name: _____

Author's Name: _____

Five Paragraph Essay
Assessment sheet

Directions: Look for the key elements of a five-paragraph essay in your partner's essay. Check off each item as you see it.

Prewriting:

	Yes	No
1. Topic Clearly Written	_____	_____
2. Three Good Main Ideas	_____	_____
3. Five supporting details for each main idea.	_____	_____

Introduction

	Yes	No
1. Thesis Statement	_____	_____
2. Three Main Ideas Written	_____	_____
3. Closing Sentence	_____	_____

Three Main Idea Paragraphs

	Yes	No
1. Each paragraph has a topic sentence.	_____	_____
2. Each paragraph has supporting details.	_____	_____
3. Each paragraph has a closing sentence.	_____	_____

Conclusion Paragraph

	Yes	No
1. Thesis Statement Summarized	_____	_____
2. Three Main Ideas Reviewed	_____	_____
3. Good Closing Sentence	_____	_____

CreateBetterWriters.com

Name:_____

Five Paragraph Essay

When you finish your essay, attach this to your work.

_____ 1. Five-Paragraph Essay Prewriting. (8 out of 10 needed to pass.)

_____ 2. Introduction Paragraph   (8 out of 10 needed to pass.)

_____ 3. Three Main Idea Paragraphs   (12 out of 15 needed to pass.)

_____ 4. Closing Paragraph   (8 out of 10 needed to pass.)

_____ 5. Completed Essay in 70 Minutes.   (4 out of 5 needed to pass.)

60 minutes or less = 5 pts.
60 – 70 minutes = 4 pts.
70 – 80 minutes = 3 pts.
80 – 90 minutes = 2 pts.
90 + minutes   = 1 pt.

Total Points – _____	Grade
	_____
Pass_____	
Keep Trying, you'll get it. _____	

Name:_____

Five Paragraph Essay

When you finish your essay, attach this to your work.

_____ 1. Five-Paragraph Essay Prewriting. (8 out of 10 needed to pass.)

_____ 2. Introduction Paragraph   (8 out of 10 needed to pass.)

_____ 3. Three Main Idea Paragraphs   (12 out of 15 needed to pass.)

_____ 4. Closing Paragraph   (8 out of 10 needed to pass.)

_____ 5. Completed Essay in 70 Minutes.   (4 out of 5 needed to pass.)

60 minutes or less = 5 pts.
60 – 70 minutes = 4 pts.
70 – 80 minutes = 3 pts.
80 – 90 minutes = 2 pts.
90 + minutes   = 1 pt.

Total Points – _____	Grade
	_____
Pass_____	
Keep Trying, you'll get it. _____	

CreateBetterWriters.com

Types of Introductions

Tell a Story: A short three to four sentence story that helps prepare the reader for the topic.

> Sentence Starters: "I'll never forget the time when…"
> "I'll always remember the time when…"
> "There was a special time in my life when…"

Attention Getter: Any statement that makes the reader want to read more. Examples include making a gross, scary, or exciting statement.

> Sentence Starters: "You'll never believe what I'm about to tell you."
> "If I could go back in time, I never would have…"
> "It was the most painful thing that I've ever felt."

Strong Opinion: Give an opinion that leads into your thesis statement. Your goal is to make people want to respond.

> Sentence Starters: "I firmly believe that…"
> "No one will ever convince me that…"
> "There is only one opinion that an intelligent person can conclude when…"

Question: Ask a question that will make the reader want to read on to find the answer.

> Sentence Starters: "Did you know …" / "Have you ever…" / "What would you think if…"

State a Fact: State a fact related to your topic that shows the importance of your thesis statement.

> Sentence Starters: "Many people would be shocked to learn that…"
> "It is surprising, but true that …"
> "Amazingly…"

Give a Statistic: Give information presented in numerical form. This is meant to prove your thesis statement is correct.

> Sentence Starters: "Statistics show…"
> "You might be surprised to learn that…"

CreateBetterWriters.com

Interesting Introductions
1

Below are introductions. Identify the type of interesting introduction by putting the name of it on the line below. The names of the introductions are in the box.

Tell a Story	Attention Getter	Strong Opinion
Question	State a Fact	Give a Statistic

Imagine! A million dollars in your pocket instantly! It might make your head spin just thinking about it. This is a problem I'd love to have. People experience this "problem" all the time as states across the country conduct lotteries every week. If I were fortunate enough to win one of these lotteries I know exactly what I'd do. I'd throw the biggest party in the world, buy my family a better house, and send my family and me to college. Just thinking about it, I can feel my mind wandering already.

_____
Type of Introduction

What would you do if you won the lottery? There are so many possibilities it is hard to narrow them down. Some people would take wonderful vacations. Others might go absolutely crazy and buy everything they've ever wanted. I might do all of those things eventually. However, if I ever won the lottery I would throw the biggest party in the world, buy my family a better house, and send my family and me to college. What an exciting event this would be.

_____
Type of Introduction

Four out of ten lottery winners are broke within a few years of winning the lottery. It might be hard to imagine that anyone could let this happen. If I won the lottery, this sure would not happen to me. I would enjoy the money now, but I would also enjoy it later and use it to make my life better. If I ever won the lottery I would throw the biggest party in the world, buy my family a better house, and send my family and me to college. This would allow me to enjoy the money now as well as later.

_____
Type of Introduction

CreateBetterWriters.com

Tell a Story	Attention Getter	Strong Opinion
Question	State a Fact	Give a Statistic

Many people who win the lottery are just plain dumb! These people win millions of dollars and, in just a few years, the money is gone. Rather than just spend like crazy, these people would be wise to take some time and think about what they should do with their new fortune. I certainly know what I would do if I won that kind of money. If I ever won the lottery I would throw the biggest party in the world, buy my family a better house, and send my family and me to college. This is a good way to have some fun and be responsible at the same time.

_____

Type of Introduction

A child opens a birthday envelope and out drops a lottery ticket. The family laughs as they joke about what a young person would do with the fortunes that could be won. The jokes turn to silence as the numbers on the ticket are compared with last nights winning numbers. Everyone stares in disbelief as they gaze at this mini-millionaire. Now imagine you were that mini-millionaire. If that were me, there are three things I'd do with the money. I would throw the biggest party in the world, buy my family a better house, and send my family and me to college. This would be a dream come true.

_____

Type of Introduction

Many lottery winners are broke within a few years of winning the lottery. It might be hard to imagine that anyone could let this happen. If I won the lottery, this sure would not happen to me. I would enjoy the money now, but I would also enjoy it later and use it to make my life better. If I ever won the lottery I would throw the biggest party in the world, buy my family a better house, and send my family and me to college. This would allow me to enjoy the money now as well as later.

_____

Type of Introduction

Answers: #1 Attention Getter, #2 Question, #3 Statistic, #4 Opinion, #5 Story, #6 Fact

Interesting Introductions
#2

Below are introductions. Identify the type of interesting introduction by putting the name of it on the line below. The names of the introductions are in the box.

Tell a Story	Attention Getter	Strong Opinion
Question	State a Fact	Give a Statistic

We could all do so much more to help make this word a better place. Even children can get involved and have a major impact on the lives of people all over the world. If you're young, don't think that you have nothing to offer because you do. Children can do as much as anyone to change the world. Examples of how children change lives every day are collecting coins for important charities, writing letters to lonely soldiers, and running recycling programs at their schools. This just shows that big changes can be made regardless of age.

_____

Type of Introduction

Children are responsible for some of the biggest improvements in the world today. It might surprise some adults to learn that kids all over the world find creative ways to make lasting impacts in the lives of those in need. It is a fact that children can do as much as anyone to change the world. Examples of how children change lives every day include collecting coins for important charities, writing letters to lonely soldiers, and running recycling programs at their schools. It is true that children can do so much to make the world a better place.

_____

Type of Introduction

Can children really make a difference in the world? You better believe they can. Children all over the world do things every day to make life better for all of us. Children make the world a better place by doing things such as collecting coins for important charities, writing letters to lonely soldiers, and running recycling programs at their schools. There is no limit to what young people can do.

_____

CreateBetterWriters.com

Type of Introduction

Tell a Story	Attention Getter	Strong Opinion
Question	State a Fact	Give a Statistic

Inside an old, broken down building sit dozens of people down on their luck. They hunch over plates of food given out for those in the city who have no place to go. Wondering if this old place can afford to keep giving free meals to the growing number of homeless who hear of this shelter, they all hope that today they'll get something to eat. Suddenly, an army of children enter carrying bags and bags of coins. The hope that these children bring is the same hope that people all over the world receive from children just like them. Children change the world everyday doing kind deeds such as raising money for important charities, writing letters to lonely soldiers, and running recycling programs at their schools. These children may be young, but they are certainly powerful.

_____

Type of Introduction

Without the help of children millions of people would starve, our soldiers would sink into deep depression, and our planet's valuable resources would dry up leaving us to freeze. This paints a shocking picture. Think about it. Children do so much to help make the world a better place. Examples of how they change the world every day include collecting coins for important charities, writing letters to lonely soldiers, and running recycling programs at their schools. It is true that children can do so much to make the world a better place.

_____

Type of Introduction

Four out of five children do things every day to help make the world a better place. It may not get a lot of attention, but children do things every day that have lasting effects on the lives of millions of people. Examples of how they change the world every day include collecting coins for important charities, writing letters to lonely soldiers, and running recycling programs at their schools. It is true that children can do so much to make the world a better place.

_____

Type of Introduction

Answers: #1 Opinion, #2 Fact, #3 Question, #4 Story, #5 Attention Getter, #6 Statistic

Name:_____

Interesting Introductions
Comma, Comma, And...

Directions: For each topic below, think of a thesis statement and three main ideas to support it. Next, write a sentence that has both your thesis statement AND your three main ideas listed.

Example: Topic: Your Best Friend

Thesis Statement: Joy is my best friend in the world.

3 Main Ideas: 1. She makes me laugh.   2. She's a good listener.   3. We have fun together.

Comma, Comma, And...

Joy is my best friend in the world because she makes me laugh, she's a good listener, and we have so much fun together.

Topic #1: Your Best Friend

Thesis Statement: Biggles is my best friend because he's been there for me since I was 4, he's a good guard dog, and he is a bit of a stinker.

3 Main Ideas:

1. He's been there for me since I was 2. He's a good guard dog.
4.
                    3. He's a bit

Comma, Comma, And...

Biggles has my best friend since I was 4 because he's a good guard dog, he makes me laugh, and he's like a brother to me.

Topic #2: A Fun Game To Play on Rainy Days

Thesis Statement: Videogames are a fun source of entertainment on Rainy Days.

3 Main Ideas:

1. They are interactive.   2. They can simulate a real life activity
                    3. VR can literally put you in a new world.

Comma, Comma, And...

Videogames are a fun sorce of entertainment on rainy days because they are interactive, they can simulate real life staring and activities, and with V.R. you can literally put your self in a new world virtually.

CreateBetterWriters.com

Topic #3: What You Want To Be When You Grow Up

Thesis Statement: _I want to be an engineer when I grow up._

3 Main Ideas:

1. _It pays well_   2. _I love building things_

3. _I want to support a family_

Comma, Comma, And...

I want to be an engineer when I grow up because I love building things, it pays well, and I want to support a family.

Topic #4: The Best Amusement Park in the World

Thesis Statement: _Galaxy's Edge is the best theme park in the world_

3 Main Ideas:

1. _There's space food_   2. _lightsabers_

3. _Theres canon star wars history behind it._

Comma, Comma, And...

Galaxy's Edge is the world's best theme park since there's tasty space food, cool lightsabers, and there is canon star wars history behind it.

Topic #5: Why You Would (or Wouldn't) Want To Be Rich

Thesis Statement: _____

_____

3 Main Ideas:

1. _____   2. _____

3. _____

Comma, Comma, And...

_____

_____

_____

Transition Words # 1

Next	First	Finally	Additionally	Second

I. Directions: Fill in the blanks with a proper transition word. Use each only once.

The ancient Egyptians had a very sophisticated process when it came to

making mummies. _____First_____, the internal organs are taken out to be washed and

dried to help prevent decomposition. _____Second_____, the organs are wrapped and placed

back in the body. _____Next_____, natron, substance that helps dry out the flesh, is packed

inside as well. _____Additionally_____, the body is washed and covered with perfumes and oils.

_____Finally_____, the body is carefully wrapped and the mummification process is complete.

II. Directions: Write a paragraph about a ~~field trip you've taken~~. Be sure to use
at least four of the five transition words.

When asked to complete this very simple task, I really struggled
and here's why. First, this is far too elementary for a 10th grader.
Second, I questioned my life's choices that lead me to writing this.
Next, I remembered I'm getting paid handsomely for this work.
Additionally, it does make my mom happy so I guess it's worth it.
Finally, it is more fun with Bigges, my dog, on my lap.

Transition Words #2

As you can see	Also	For example	Furthermore	Lastly

I. Directions: Fill in the blanks with a proper transition word. Use each only once.

Male emperor penguins are excellent fathers. _For example_, they

will stand on an egg for weeks without food just to protect their child from the cold.

Furthermore, the male emperor penguin will allow the female to leave

during this time to find food for herself. _Lastly_, being aware of the dangers

of the wind, he will huddle together with other dads to help block other eggs from

the dangerous wind. _Also_, only when the egg has hatched and the child

is safely in the mother's care will the male emperor penguin take care of himself.

As you can see, the male emperor penguin is a fine example of

fatherhood for all species to follow.

II. Directions: Think of a subject you've studied in school. Write a paragraph
        about it. Be sure to use at least four of the five transition words.

Being told about these transition words is somewhat
insulting to some one of my I.Q. For example, I have a 4.0 grade
average yet I sitting here writing this paragraph. Furthermore, I work
really hard every day and I'm still doing what you asked. As you can see,
I'm only doing this for cash. Also it makes you happy so it's worth it
I suppose.

Transition Words #3

Next	First	Finally	Additionally	Second
As you can see	Also	For example	Furthermore	Lastly

I. Directions: Fill in the blanks with a proper transition word.

There are many things you can do to help make the world a better place. __For example__, you can begin a recycling program at your school and encourage everyone to recycle unwanted paper. __Also__, you could organize a clothing donation program. __Additionally__, you can ask people to donate clothes that their children have out grown. There are many people who can use these items. __Furthermore__, it will make you feel good about yourself for doing it. __Next__, another great thing you can do for the world is to encourage people to save their change for the homeless shelters in your area. __As you can see__, there are many great things you can do to help those in need.

II. Directions: Write a paragraph about something a young person can do to make the world a better place. Be sure to use at least four of the transition words.

As a young adult, there typicaly isn't alot one can do for the community that would make a world wide difference. For example, many foundatrons, clubs, and other social groups who try and make a change only effect the people who are part of them. That being said, what ← I thought it was good. could help the world change? Simply be selfless! Help others if they lost their pencil, have a question on their homework, etc, As you can see, Kindness is not just the key to making the world a better place, additionally it is the key to making a more social and unique sociaty.

Transition Words #4
Persuasive Writing

In my opinion	In addition	I believe	In my experience
Consequently	Although	Therefore	Despite

I. Directions: Fill in the blanks with a proper transition word from the box.

_____ there should be more skateboard parks built in our city.

_____, kids are going to find a place to skateboard whether we like it of not.

_____, we should provide safe areas where they can ride without becoming a

danger to others. _____ the growing number of skateboard users, there continues to

be few places they can go to have their fun. _____, they do it in areas that are

hazardous for themselves or others. _____, boarders have been begging for

their own place for years, little has been done. _____, I've found that when you

give young people safe alternatives to gangs, drugs, and other harmful activities, they have a lot

better opportunity to become responsible adults. _____, building more

skateboard parks is not a luxury, it's a necessity.

II. Directions: Write a paragraph. Try to persuade someone to do something to
improve a condition at home or at school. Be sure to use at least four of the
transition words or phrases from the box.

_____

_____

_____

_____

_____

_____

_____

Transition Sentences

When writing a five-paragraph essay, one of the first things that you do is find three main ideas. These main ideas should be related somehow.

Transition Sentences: In this worksheet, you are going to look at a few transition strategies. These are the kinds of transitions you should be making whenever you write an essay. Read the tips below, then find the transitions in the paragraphs. Next, return to an essay that you have already written and try to add similar transitions to your essay.

Tips: 1. Use words from one sentence to transition to another sentence.
        2. Use transition words to connect ideas from one paragraph to another.
            Examples: Speaking of...   Regarding...

I. Directions: Find the transition sentences in the paragraphs below. Explain to a partner which tip from above was used.

Topic: Why Saturday is my favorite day of the week
Three Main Ideas: 1. Sleeping in   2. Hang out with friends   3. Family Night

Saturdays are so great because it is the only day of the week I get to sleep in. After being out all night on Friday, not worrying about the alarm going off makes the last few hours of sleep more special. There are days when I might wake up, but stay in bed until my body tells me it's ready. Other days, it takes a bolt of sunshine directly into my eyes to get me out of bed. Therefore, sleeping in late is a great way to spend a Saturday.

Speaking of great ways to spend a Saturday, hanging out with my friends is another reason why I love Saturdays. I usually get a call from my best friend, Jeff, at about ten. We'll meet at the park and play football for an hour or two. Then we might go over someone's house and play video games. Sometimes we'll go to the mall. What usually makes Saturdays fun is not the things we do, it's that we're doing it together. Therefore, having fun with friends makes Saturdays so much fun.

Having fun with friends may be fun, but my family's Family Night is the most fun a person can have on a Saturday. Sometimes my Uncle Jim comes over and he teaches me how to work on engines. Then we eat pizza and play games. We'll watch a video or just play music while talking. There hasn't been a Family Night yet that wasn't a good time.

II. Use these transition tips to add transitions to the paragraphs of an essay that you have already written.

Narrative
Writing

Definition:

_____

_____

_____

_____

_____

_____

_____

Persuasive
Argument

Definition:

_____

_____

_____

_____

_____

_____

_____

_____

Problem / Solution

Definition:

_____

_____

_____

_____

_____

_____

_____

Cause and Effect

Definition:

_____

_____

_____

_____

_____

_____

_____

_____

Research Report

Definition:

_____

_____

_____

_____

_____

_____

_____

Made in the USA
San Bernardino, CA
07 June 2020